Middlesex
Triplet

MARCIE NATALY

ISBN 978-1-0980-3725-3 (paperback)
ISBN 978-1-0980-3726-0 (digital)

Christian Faith Publishing
832 Park Avenue
Meadville, PA 16335
www.christianfaithpublishing.com

Printed in the United States of America

Success

O God, Father of Heaven, that I would not fail thee
In my dreams,
In my play,
In my work,
And in my way.
Oh, for today,
May you say
I am here to stay.
We have longings, but what could we want more than you?
My Poems are not written for the sake of rhyme
It is words you have given me in time.
Oh, for the story behind them,
Let the words on the heart of your daughter here on earth below.
Written here in stow
And may they forever set all hearts for you aglow.

(Miss Marcie Lindquist,
completed February 25, 1994)

God Speaks

My love for you is abounding.
My sacrifice for you astounding.
There is no big or small gift that I won't give
If it is in my will.
Tell the little ones that Jesus loves them.
Tell the grown ones He adores them.
He's knocking at the door to your heart.
Do you hear? Will you let him in?
There's nothing he can't handle,
No problem big or small.
He says, "Try my shoulders to lean on.
They're strong enough for you.
Weary world, come to me.
Let me set your soul free."
Begin, begin again, be born, be born again,
Spiritually, not physically.
A second birth is what he calls for
To confess your sins to him and everlasting life will
Be his promise today and forever more.

(Marcie B. Lindquist,
written January 1992)

I Thirst

Drink of the heavenly sky.
Drink of the waters that never run dry.
Be penitent with God.
Be patient with the path He has given you to trod.
Smell the myrrh of your soul.
Drink from the one who can make you whole.
Bind his wounds up, oh Christian peoples of this Earth,
And He will show you how much you were worth.
Two thousand years ago, He died on a tree
Just to give you life and set your soul free.
When life on this Earth for me is o're,
Swing low, sweet savior, to bring me home to that eternal shore

Amen.

(Marcie B. Lindquist)

Bible

I go to the Bible when I'm sad.
I go to the Bible when I'm glad.
I go to the Bible when I'm mad.
I go to the Bible when I've been had.
Speak to me, Lord, from your precious Word.
For in you, I know I have been heard.
You come when the whole world shuts me out.
With this, I know beyond the shadow of a doubt.
Fill me with your spiritual rebirth,
And tell me just how much I was worth.
No Earthly king is as great as you.
I worship you in my heart and soul anew.
With each prayer, I know you care,
And you truly are there.
So we need not despair.

(Marcie Lindquist)
Letter to Rev. Charles Stanley

Dear Rev. Charles Stanley,

It was my good pleasure to listen to your wonderful tape from a sermon series on Unmet Needs called "The Basics." It was this tape on the three basic unmet needs that so deeply touched my life and those I've played it too. I have also listened to your son, Andy Stanley. The one on character. It is true we live in a society where achievement is placed above godly character and the family. Enclosed I have written a poem, which includes themes from both your sermons. I hope you will read and enjoy it. It is my hope someday to get my poetry, of which this is just one, published.

Please respond if you get a chance.

Sincerely,
Miss Marcie B. Lindquist

It has been my good pleasure to listen and watch Dr. Rev. Charles and Rev. Andy Stanley. I listened to Dr. Charles Stanley's message on basic unmet needs. In this tape and sermon, he reflects on how important it is for people to have basic needs met. How if they're not met it leads us to look elsewhere to get this sense of belonging, competence, and worth met. In his sermon, I learned we need not look elsewhere if our needs aren't met or weren't met during childhood. We can go to God to have this sense of these three basic unmet needs. In my upbringing my parents for the most part were there. They occasionally escaped the routine of parenthood in their newspaper reading and television. So I reflect on this sermon and the one his son Andy Stanley his son preached "Character" in a poem entitled "Needs."

Sincerely,
Miss Marcie B. Lindquist

Needs

Thank you, Lord, that you are always available,
And for our unmet needs, you are always capable.
With you, we have a sense of belonging and of worth.
You showed us this by your coming to this earth
In a virgin birth.

I have learned today that we can do anything God wants us to do.
So in the miles ahead, we need not fret but go to you instead.
For soon, the miles will be few to trod,
And in your sweet heaven, we will be with you, Lord.
So give us that sense of belonging, worthiness, and competence.
Build our character, you know, Lord, the ability to do
What is right despite the personal cost.
For in you, we are not lost.
We thank you for good looks if they can be used for your glory,
For you are more concerned with what goes on in the heart,
More than achievement or material gain.
You made this evident by your life on earth; it was so plain.
So bless those who preach the gospel and your message to us.
For in you dear God, triune, we put our trust.

(Marcie Lindquist Nataly)

Lent Poem

Lord, as I pray and read your
Word, show me your admonition.
Examine my every ambition
When we say we have no sin
And think we win;
Present your slate of those enemies I hate
The lack of compassion or love
To those that have wronged me and
To the ones I love,
And see if there be
Any way that I want that isn't according to thee.
It's not a holy amnesia of the past you want
Or the wrong to go unpunished or unrepented.
You want the poison in my heart to be lifted from me,
For I have to remember it is by grace,
Given to me after I repented that you set my soul free.

(Marcie B. Lindquist)

Remember:

IN him we have redemption through His blood, the forgiveness of sins, according to the riches of His Grace. (Ephesians 1:7)

In Him you also trusted, after you heard the word of truth, the gospel of your salvation in whom also having believed, you were sealed with the Holy Spirit of promise. (Ephesians 1:13)

The eyes of your understanding being enlightened that you may know what is the hope of his calling, what are the riches of the Glory of His inheritance in the Saints. (Ephesians 1:18)

Which He worked in Christ when He raised Him from the dead and seated Him at His right hand in the Heavenly places. (Ephesians 1:20)

Another Day

The boughs above
And the branches below
Echo their hello.
Snow falls down
All around.
As your breath continues to speak
Another day
Hooray! Hooray!
For the mild and the meek.

My inner self
Has a gulf
That only you can fill
Try as I might
For the conversation to others plight.
They don't understand and see me in the height
That you God do.
So I run to you
Penetrate me, O God, and show me thy will.

(Marcie B. Lindquist,
poem written February 23, 1994)

Definition of some words: Gulf is a deep hollow in the earth, but here it is my soul. A chasm.
Plight is to engage in.

Noah

Oh, my God, though art true,
You have brought to light Noah's ark anew;
On top of Mount Ararat, it's hue,
Beneath the skies of love so blue.
Who could imagine that five thousand years
Later, it would be in plain view.
Your love for us has never changed
Your rainbow after the flood still remains.
Draw closer still I can hear you say,
I will show you more another day
To believe in me sight unseen is greater still,
To read your Holy Bible and pray, this is your will.
Spread the good news of the Gospel is for ours to heed.
To love one another in thought, word, and deed.
I love you, God, Father, Son, and Holy Spirit. Amen.

(Marcie B. Lindquist,
written after viewing a program on the
discovery of Noah's Ark, January 1993)

Hail Our Christmas King

Oh, Lord, I see the trumpet ornament hanging on my tree,
And I am reminded that you are a King.
Oh, Lord, I see the glistening powered snow adorned
On Heaven's earth below,
And I am reminded of the great things you bring.

Thinking of you every minute of the day,
Reaching to you and in our souls pray.
In the world's eyes, we may have no lofty place.
Some of us may even hold disgrace.
A follower of you, they say we are.
They know not this world holds a temporary space
And in Heaven, Lord, we will as we do down here your power embrace.

There are friends, Lord, who warm our hearts.
True kindred spirits, God, who see our needs and fill them,
Without a plea; and as for me, Lord, you know me oh so well.
In your presence, Lord, I like others to tell you wish for
Us to dwell. In you, I know I do, Lord. Amen.

(Marcie Lindquist Nataly)

Tell Me of You, God

He speaks to me through the breeze,
Blowing on me and in the trees.
He speaks to me in my heart,
And beside me and in me, I know He dwells and will never part.
He's bringing me down some promised road.
For this I praise him, glory to God.
It is my good pleasure to be part of his abode.
I do not question His mode.
And with a struggle, sometimes I give Him my heavy load.
So bow down your soul and let Him in it seep and seep.
And when our soul weeps,
It is Him who our being will keep.
Remember if the road at times seems too steep,
And we wonder what life we will reap,
Trust in Him it will all be well.
And although time sometimes will only tell,
It is eternally in Him we dwell.

In Christ Jesus,
My Lord and Savior

(Marcie Lindquist Nataly)

The Voice Unheard,
the Heartbeat Unfelt

Many are the stars of the night.
Many are the wars by day.

Cease-fire, cease-fire.

Do we die tomorrow?
Shall we live today?

Oh, impoverished nations,
How shall we help thee?
Will we become one in the same?

Wars within the family,
Wars without.

Gang wars, street wars, drug wars, yes, there is even more; the war
of all generations; the war of the unborn musician, the war of the
unborn doctor, with the cure for cancer or AIDS.

Twenty-eight million, they say since they've legalized these atrocities.

Oh, for today, let there be one life saved.

Let there be one more doctor to lay down his weapon
Let there be one more mother who will respect that human sacred
life inside her.

Most legislators don't care for these most helpless and vulnerable of society who have no right to vote.

"Pro-choice, pro-choice," they say;
"Pro-life, pro-life," in God we pray.

(Marcie B. Lindquist Nataly,
written summer 1991)

Child Abuse

Let the children cry, let them be comforted.
Why do they cry mother?
Why do they cry, Father?
Is it because of you that they mourn?
Because their bodies and souls are torn?
How many blows have they been given?
How many bruises or broken bones?
When will the system learn they must have other permanent homes?
"Let the little children come to me," says Jesus, our God and Savior.
Oh, children, He will never strike you, and He does not waver.
Lord, heal their wounds emotionally and physically.
This may take years because of their many fears.
Through it all, you will get through somehow.
No tear is shed without your Lord knowing.
So when you go to bed, know that one day, He shall wipe all the tears
dry, but until then, pretend
That He is drying them now, oh let there be a human hand to reach
To dry your tears and let love of body soul and mind teach!
Protect the children, dear Lord. Protect the children!

(Marcie B. Lindquist,
written after viewing a documentary on story of
Adam Man, summer or spring of 1993)

Hope for Tomorrow

Sand blows relentlessly,
But the sun still shines bright,
My dreams for tomorrow hang in that light.

In the view of the ocean, the whole world encompasses me.
The strength of the earth uplifts me.
Will but the best of dreams be mine to have?
And the peace and love they grace never ever die.
Fly, seagull, fly

(Marcie B. Lindquist Nataly,
written summer 1982)

Peace & Love
Fritz, Marcie
and Jacob

Betrayal

The tear beats a drum of loneliness.
The men have left their uncaring mark.
A fool's game won by none.
If only God could give me the one
That cared for all of me.
The wanting of what lacks to keep
Them mine.
Love stained to the bitter end.
No man has done his part.
In a modern world, the woman is torn.
Between sheets of boredom, the dawn arises.
Lonely and abandoned, she forever wants
To leave this earth.
God, however, has given her some love,
For herself. Things she wishes to know about herself,
Beyond the commonly used beauty.

(Marcie B. Lindquist,
written summer 1984)

Husbandman

Oh, Lord, who can I go to with my deepest concern and fears, but you!
Who will see my view the way you do?
You say you know how I feel, you see what I see the way I see it.
The look these men have given me, I've seen it before.
The way he gives me that forced grin and then sticks out his tongue.
In the end, you will see that they are the ones who will be undone.
A perverted evil man I know from far off. His look will not go
unchecked, nor will his way be powerful long.
For it is you sweet Jesus who will hunt them down.
It is you who wears that Heavenly crown.
Their secret motives will be brought to light,
And proper punishment will be their plight.
So bring to me those, Lord, whom I can truly trust:
If there be any but you.
And give me discernment that is not blind,
For an omniscient Lord like you is one of a kind.

(Marcie B. Lindquist)

Dad

A father you have been to me, oh so true,
Rare, loving, caring, and kind: that's you.
Never has it crossed my mind there would be
Better than mine.
For thirty-six years, you've fathered my soul,
And you don't even look like it has taken its toll.
Though the words may be few,
And the visits speak their shifting breeze:
Father-and-daughter times we do our thoughts weave
And cleave to render no more thoughts undone
For a memory of jubilant life with you, God, has spun.

(Marcie B. Lindquist,
written for Father's Day, 1993)

Mom

Your touch is gentle, strong, and kind,
A rare pearl with color so sublime.
Always, my thoughts about you are dear;
And at night my prayers for you are ever near.
Speak of your dreams, my mother, your mother's child,
Or have they already come true in a manner so mild.
Forever is a word that describes your love,
Not plundering or thundering but
Gracefully flowing as a dove
With each decade brings a world at times so strange.
However, my daughterly love for you and how deeply I value
You will never ever change.
Peace, be still, my mother, peace be still.

(Marcie B. Lindquist,
written fall 1992)

Janet

Janet is a dream,
An older sister that gleams.
Over the years, she's grown and cared
For a husband, a son, and oh what fun
To see them up here on a lake where
The family cottage begun.
Could we spare her this older sister of mine,
Only to her husband and son I think.
She's articulate, sensitive, caring, and adorned
With more beauty than many a women previously born.
Many a rose could be compared with such inner and outer
Beauty as this,
And if I might say, I miss
Not seeing her more often this.
So with a sisterly kiss
I wish you, my sister Janet, and brother-in-law Ira,
And nephew Reed a life full of bliss.

Love,

(Marcie B. Lindquist Nataly,
written summer of 1993)

Reed

A nephew is one whom your sister bore,
Someone whom you really adore,
Have not known all you've been through in life thus far.
Your mother used to say, "Just keep wishing on a star,
Makes no difference where you are, your dreams come true.
Hope someday, if not already, that will be of you!"

Love,
Auntie Marcie

IT'S OFF TO SCHOOL — Six six-year old Maynard
Mark and Marcia Lindquist, children of Mr. and Mrs. Walter
quist, 35 Euclid avenue, Maynard. Children entered first
Green Meadow School, yesterday morning.

Gary

A big brother is like no other,
Shoulders to carry me when I was young,
Laughter to share as my life begun.
Sorrow to bear as my journeys though life hung.
I never asked if you were there
Because I know you really did care.
Miles and miles separate us now.
Big brothers still get through somehow.
Confidence and assuredness are in your voice,
But to know you better as a brother is my choice.
We have such a short life in this world.
Joys untold is for ours to unfold.
So no need to ask me if I'm really there.
Just know that I truly, truly do care.

(Marcie B. Lindquist)

OFF TO SCHOOL — for six-year old Maynard triplets.
and Marcia Lindquist, children of Mr. and Mrs. Wallace
t, 36 Espie avenue, Maynard. Children entered first gre
n Meadow School, yesterday morning. (Staff

Sweet Sis

If I have not the courage to carry on,
You will let me lean on you.
Nothing more alike in physique,
Cursed be the note that parts our tune.
For with every cell we grew,
In the likeness of every gene,
We nestled and became two human beings:
You and I.

Our hearts did beat in the same blanket of warmth
Through which the blood of life from our mother's womb
Fed us.
Nothing could part us then.
Like a two-edged sword, we protect one another,
Each side uniquely established,
One being you the other I.

Fair-haired and blue-eyed,
We look at each other in admiration.
We will take each step in life,
Glancing over at each other
To share the new experiences with joy.

And if by chance life's cruelty has surrounded you,
I will fly down like an eagle,
To fly you high about the sorrow,
For you are more than a mirror image of my being,
You are my living identical triplet.

(Marcie B. Lindquist,
copyright 1985, written fall 1985)

Triplet Brother

The altruistic brother triplet twin that looks within.
Quiet, gentle, strong, and true,
He'll do anything for you.
Knit together from a place within,
God knows this redheaded brother would be my twin.
Will he be a farmer, and oceanographer, an engineer, or something altogether more?
There is something churning deep within his core.
There is forbearance in my fraternal brother's care;
Reach out, reach out to our sisterly stare.
Do not let life come crushing down.
But if it does, remember there are many up in Heaven
Who bear a crown.
Full reward, full reward for being eyes of blue
Altruistic triplet brother that's you.

(Marcie B. Lindquist)

Middlesex Triplet

In the most longing cravings of my soul
I wish I were in the Savior's arms pure and whole.

The memory of what it was like to not have a complete vagina
Through and through, the dream of it being hard as a rock,
Clawing at it to scrape it out so I could be complete from within and
out.

Torture there, loneliness and despair.
Surely, others have sought my prayer
To have a love eternal reaching to me
Arms outstretched, to not just stare at his sketch.
He would love me as I am;
He has made me surely, I don't know why, but this was his plan.

I'm not a cookie cutter of womanhood,
But the children I have understood.
To be a woman is in the heart.
To breed through the womb is just the start.

Some can complete this task so strong,
Others God has destined to carry on.
It's He that has made you through and through,
Mind, body, soul, and whomever you are beautiful too.

(Marcie B. Lindquist Nataly,
written spring 1993)

Satu

Satu is my friend,
Like a little sister to the end.
From a land that my grandfather knew,
Here to visit the skies so blue.
Children and animals have sensed her love,
Free-spirited and loyal as the angels above.
She understands these thoughts of mine,
And when we sit to unwind,
I know she accepts me as one of her own kind.
Finnish-descent through and through.
Young, beautiful, and innocent too.
When we're together, we laugh and laugh.
Oh, the joys of having a friend so dear!
I hope we will remain close friends forever from year to year!

Love,
Marcie B. Lindquist

(*Sisko* is Finnish for sister,
written spring of 1993)

Maureen

She was my cousin, a good mother, a loving daughter
A gracious sister.
Oh, that we could be with her!
Taken so young,
Not by a gun,
Or old age after much life of fun,
But by a disease
That victims do not often heed.
Her date was not sober behind the wheel.
With this danger it was hard to deal
By God's grace, we go on,
With each new dawn,
For He brings hope for tomorrow
To wipe away our sorrow.

(Marcie B. Lindquist,
written January 6, 1994)

Sweden

My sweet, sweet Sweden,
No sweeter was there even found in the Garden of Eden.
My green-eyed gem,
A dew drop purring,
My love enduring.
Sleep, my precious one,
My gray-furred friend,
For my love for you there is no end.

(Marcie B. Lindquist,
written January 1992)

No Better Love

My beloved art mindful of things of God.
My beloved is mightier than ten thousand stallions.
His hand is like a shepard's hand upon his sheep,
More tender is his touch.
My Lord knoweth and art mindful of a woman's needs.
You have said to me that my face is like a mountain,
Side in the springtime where the lilies grow and the sun shines.
You face is as the stars of the universe in their night
Splendor; no one shines as great as thee.
My remembrance of you on the blood-splotched cross
Bearing my pain, my sin, my toil, my heartache, oh,
There are not just one but a few.
"Still, the best is yet to come," says one whom I desire.
Far be it for me to argue with one who my soul loveth.
But to love you is purer still. I seek the purest wine,
To drink of the Heaven's gate.
You seek out my heart for a better fate.
Be still, my God, be still, I will not fail thee.

(Marcie B. Lindquist,
written January 1991 or 1992)

True love

No better man have I met in life,
For He has in His heart a good God
Who accepts with sin and has no strife.
This man I've deeply loved, how
Much I have not realized over the years
Till now. His stately beauty is
Becoming, forthcoming. Do not delay.
Hail righteousness, hail sovereignty of God.
To God be all the glory for creating this man
Who has so deeply touched my life.
And it is my forever wish that I should be his wife.

(Marcie B. Lindquist,
written on January 1992)

Despair

O God, how long will I suffer here on earth!
I cry in whispers to you, Lord God, for my heart is breaking.
I remember David's fingers wiping away my tears,
And he's no longer here.
I cry out to you, Lord Jesus, in the night
That you could wipe away my tears,
And I could see you in full sight.
A friend has said to me, "Let your heart not carry on about Him,"
Who I wish to marry.
For he has told you how he feels.
But when I see him, my heart hopes and gladdens.
I cry because my heart saddens at the thought of not having him.
He has sent me no material gift except friendly flowers;
It's the way I feel when I'm around him when were together.
I feel joy that wells up in my soul.
Attraction physically, emotionally, mentally, and spiritually.
Words cannot utter all that I feel toward him.
The king's heart is in the hand of the Lord.
You turn it whatever way you will.
Lord, good God, do not take away this man I love.
May I find a place in his heart as he has in mind.
For feelings for him are never out of line.
Bend down your ear to me, eternal Father of Heaven.
You know me better than I can even try.
God, you are saying to me that you have a plan,
And it may be that only you know whether he is the right
Soul mate to me of a man.
O God, let me not be forsaken again.

Heartbreaking once, heartbreaking twice, and again and again.
What is it that lets me in hindsight see that the other men weren't the
right ones for me
I will cling to You by and by. I try,
Lord Jesus, to seek utmost your heavenly kingdom.
I wait, trying to be patient. I wait to see your perfect will.
Oh, Lord, you know it is a hard thing for my soul to be still.
So I utterly abandon everything to you.
And in time, I will say that my soul grew.
A movie I saw says your will becomes our heart's desire.
Why did he say to watch this movie?
Why did he stare at me that way the other night?
As you know, Jesus, when He's around, I can't let him out of my sight.
My friend Lord says that I'm reading into things,
That I'm seeing what I want to see.
That it's not really there.
I hear Lord and want to know the truth.
Let it not be part of a scheme
That only the lowliest of me would dream.
To lead a woman on and on,
Then to turn around and be gone.
Surely, this isn't the type of man he is.
My soul wrenches with pain of his rejections,
But on reflection,
He has been kind, although dubious about me from time to time.
Words have I spoken to him on paper to bind him near.
What has it done but shed these numerous tears?
He has not betrayed me like the others.
He has only wanted for me the best.
Why does he not see me as compatible?
I thought I saw the longing of me in his eye.
What do I do but try and try?
Is my youth against me is it my past?
Those things which have left some aghast.
Oh, Lord, closer to him I want to be.

Not to own him or domineer him but to be his best friend,
And to listen to him when he calls my name.
It is you we want to have the glory and fame.
I'm tired now, and, Lord, I shall go to bed.
And on your eternal breast, I shall rest my weary head.

(Marcie B. Lindquist,
written 1993 late winter early spring)

Mere Bride's Delight

Oh, child, wilt thou see
What I have in store for thee.
Winter snow or spring's delight,
I will guide thee with my might.
As the night grows nigh on and on,
My true love will rise to preach in the morning's dawn. It is great honor to hear his words.
They convey your sweetness, Lord, your song, like that of my favorite chickadee bird.
The Lord is my shepherd. He gives me words that are hidden in my heart.
And from his side, I know I will never part.
You know me, Lord, better than I can even tell. Let me hear a wedding bell.
Nearer in you Lord I want to be.
Tell this to my loved ones and set their souls free.
If ever a man should come to me, let it be this one whom my soul loves. Although I know it's my Lord who is the answer to every cry of my heart. Make it crystal-clear to us, Lord, and that we would know whether we're meant for each other.
When I hear my true love's voice, my heart sings in rejoice.
As the violin needeth the bow to play,
So my heart needeth Him to sing and cherish his wedding ring.
Not that in the ring I find my bliss.

If he would just give me a kiss and speak what's on his heart for me.
Surely, there is nothing wrong in that; and if there is a way in your plan, oh, Lord, let it ever be so grand,
And let it be said that we in this life we'll be wed.

Love,
Marcie.

(Written November 1993)

Rape

This body is so fragile,
So vulnerable, uncertain of danger.
You are so mighty and powerful and able to deliver.
Put your strong arms about me, Lord,
That I may never leave your sight or side.
Touch within me, this weary damsel, her soul,
Her mind, her fear, ever be so near,
And I will abide under your wings;
In you will I trust.
Oh, to never again be the victim of a perverse thrust!

(Marcie B. Lindquist)

For You Alone, O Lord, Make Me to Dwell in Safety

I stare at the pain
Of the emotional scars that remain,
Soaring to new heights of my being;
Pierced, my soul, by nights of deceiving;
Though I kept on believing
In a God who did dwell
In my heart and tell
Of things that were worth receiving.
The pain laid me bare
To a God who did care
And it's in his arms I'm now healing.
Trust in the Lord: trust the Lord,
For He is good!

(Marcie B. Lindquist)

Healing

I will both lie down in peace and sleep
You are my star, Lord. You are my rock.
I close my eyes, and I see dark.
I think of you as a star in the night.
When you first look at the night, it looks so lonely and forsaken.
All is black.
But like the faithful God you are, you appear
Like you promise, you embark in the night.
Your creation does not emulate you.
It does, however, speak in part of the wonderful God that you are.
As your wind blows softly through the trees, it somehow whispers
You hear me. You really, really do.
So hear my prayer, O Lord, every great and little prayer.
Intercede for me, dear Jesus. Petition all of Heaven to pray.
To gently heal my dear sister, O Lord God, the sister of my soul, to
let her sleep tonight as she's never slept before in a gentle peace that
exceeds the rainfall in the night.
Oh, encompass us with your love, ever so bright.
Sleep, my mother whose wisdom is beyond compare,
Whose experience has brought us safely through our worldly fare.

Lest we toss and turn all night
And be overcome with fright,
See us safely through, dear Emmanuel,
Through our plight.
To love us, to guide us, to shelter us through the storm.
Under your wings, we are preserved,
And we are so blessed with your salvation
That we did not deserve!

(Marcie B. Lindquist)

An American

Lord, as I hear the Olympics come to an end
And the national anthem of Norway play,
I ask where it is I feel at home.
Would I feel more at home in Sweden or Finland
Of whose descent I physically am,
Or France where my descent further rolls, or to Canada
Where my grandmother was born?
I reflect back to that glorious morn,
Where I swam and looked up to view
My blessed American flag
Aglow with stars and stripes and freedom passed before me
Fought years ago:
And although some, we are ashamed to call American,
Truly an American I am with a kindred spirit toward the blood
Countries from which ethnicity I stand.

(Marcie B. Lindquist)

Hockey

What is it about this little puck
That makes these men run so amuck?
It would be fine if all they did was
Skate and flick that hockey stick to score,
But on there is so much needless more.
They fight to an unglorious height.
They perch; they lurch
At one another, a cut, a bruise, a gash of how they bash.
You'd think they were off to war as they cry for more,
Not in it for sport,
Or what of this lot.
As for me, I'd rather see Nancy Kerrigan skate triple-toe
Leaps of glee.

(Marcie B. Lindquist,
written December 1993 or January 1994)

CPSIA information can be obtained
at www.ICGtesting.com
Printed in the USA
BVHW031520040422
633291BV00004B/176